These Stunted
Jersey
Pines

NORMA PAUL

Order this book online at www.trafford.com
or email orders@trafford.com

Most Trafford titles are also available at major online book retailers.

Printed in the United States of America.

ISBN: 978-1-4669-9653-3 (sc)
ISBN: 978-1-4669-9655-7 (hc)
ISBN: 978-1-4669-9654-0 (e)

Library of Congress Control Number: 2013941117

Trafford rev. 05/22/2013

 www.trafford.com

North America & international
toll-free: 1 888 232 4444 (USA & Canada)
phone: 250 383 6864 ✦ fax: 812 355 4082

Acknowledgements

For Dick, my one true love, who supported my many attempts at becoming a woman, who made me strong, who made me laugh, who taught me how to open myself to sensuality and joy.

For Karen, Gus, Valerie, Laurie, Jo-Eva, Joyce, Brett who have taught me how to be a mother through all its wins and losses.

For Ronnie, Susan, Tom, Ray, Barry, Bob for giving your love to my loves.

For Anada, Jennifer, Stefanie, Catherine, Leandra, Meredie, Erika, Brian, Richard, Harry, Kia, Jil, Emma, Joel, Ethan for all your giving ways.

A Cold Morning
for September

The day began before the sky paled—a
cold morning for September.
Stars stood waiting for light
to obliterate their presence.
Distant planes droned among them
a reminder that life sings
above these stunted Jersey pines.

The quiet morning held
comforting moments of
close-quartered rhythm
established eons ago
during intermission.

Dancing together was never as
free-flowing, as breath-taking
as those early tentative steps
around our buzz of conversation.

This morning—each morning—began
again with that astonishing recognition.

Daily Paper

We always had the local newspaper
in our house when
I was a kid.
I'd be sent to the corner to pick up
the Buffalo Evening News—Blue Star
edition—three cents.
I'd read the headlines
walking back. I felt
a child of privilege in spite of
cardboard insoles
my father had shaped into
my year-old black oxfords
while he was home in between
his ship's drydock and the next call for
a digging crew for the WPA.
Reading drew us close to Wrong-Way
Corrigan and Wendell Wilkie,
Joe Louis, the Lindbergh baby,
Roller Derby queens, the Bisons,
Wallis Simpson. We marveled
that a mother had named her baby girl
other than Mary or Joan way back then,
linking fame from then on
with exclusiveness.

Homeschooled

I learned the Blues from my mother.
I mean Mama taught me the Blues
Taught me the meaning of the Blues—the wailing
Yes the Blues wail. They moan.
My mother moaned.
Her silent choking cacophony
Wailed down her cold-creamed cheeks
I pretended I didn't see
She pretended too.
We dropped no words into the
Deep gulf between us.
Radio waves blew Bessie's mournful melancholy
    through me.
Motionless I held my arms at my sides
Listening to Bessie
Fingering her words up the scale and
Down again
Throbbing her words through her throat in
Mounting sibilance.
Sliding them between her
Compressed lips
Silk through satin.

All Through My Young Childhood

All through my young childhood,
after hearing that guardian angels
watch over children to protect them,
I wondered with an edge of bitterness
where my very own guardian angel could be,
sure she was not protecting me.

Unprotected, I thought I was not good enough
maybe not child enough at the age of eight
to deserve such an angel—
old enough now to take care of myself.
Or was my angel in charge
of other children too,
other needier children,
so could not fit me into her
daily allotted time for such chores.

To take care of myself,
I would repent of that day's evil,
determine to start over again the next morning.
The next morning would find such resolutions
sorely tested, then abandoned to the
"never mind" philosophy
such a child learns to develop.

After many such lessons dearly learned,
one startling day that negligent guardian
hissed in my ear, "What are you waiting for?
Come On! Get out of here!"

Day-Lily

A world unreeled before her eyes when
first they lighted on your slow brown study.

Did you size her up as easy conquest as
your hands bid the day-lily open to the sun
only to mock in withdrawal of warmth and
shining with the turning of your back?

She stands motionless. Her head does not droop.
Her roots plunge deep.
Day-lily! Thrust your stamen high!

When one day you turn again
whose world then will be unreeled?
For is not the sun diluted
as the day winds down to the west?

A Man Who Moves Me

There is a thoughtful man who moves me,
Moves my mind to pursue thought.
No longer content to let words drift in and out of
Consciousness in familiar flowing channel,
I cut across to his island of Questioning.

There is a passionate man who moves me.
He moves passions early dampened by a
Stream of disdain for inept innocence.
Now Passion flares into bloom with the
Surge of Indian Summer,
Thrust hot through the center of my being.

There is a man who sweetly woos me without intent.
Lips part to savor dew held in afternoon roses
In care to crush not this fleeting bouquet.

There is a gentle man who moves me
Without stirring, without touching.
He will not be stirred by my touch
Although I melt by his.
My touch merely tickles his tolerant godly humor.
He kindly kisses my nose.

It's absurd to die from a kiss on the nose.
There is a man who moves me—to die.

Bohemian Child

Listen ponder be still
Listen listen ponder be still
—Eight o'clock bedtime Now I lay me down to sleep
Dark winter Light summer
Still dark summer morning Pray the Lord my soul to keep
Empty bed
She drags a string along the ground lifts it into the air
Calico kitten jumps and paws until *they* appear
Shivering in pre-dawn damp, their voices shaking
Scold the girl back back from white blooming cherry tree
Back from delicious May morning back into their cocoon of
dismal space raw floorboards laid on packed earth
Mayflies swarming in the fetid air.
If I should die before I wake—
Pray the Lord my soul to take—
Back into narrow white wrought iron bed.
Wait for suspicion of dawn.

Flecks of Fools' Gold

Heading for St. Louis, travelers pulsing east
race down Route Forty-four. Brick sentinels at
Webster Grove guard against incursion into
insular lives of Midwestern piety.
Behind one forbidding façade
restive brown eyes scan the ceaseless flow.

Trembling, chill, one lone driver feels the
piercing raw desire which penetrates
Missouri's petrified red clay
compels a hard right turn on the wheel.

Motor idling, the seductive lure to
return to the fevered game churns.
Summer detours sing idyllic. But time is
lost. So much time is lost.

In summer's mist a writhing silver-green stream
turns up a stone to catch the light in
flecks of fools' gold.
Let summer lie. Release the oak's brown leaves to
crackle and fly down Forty-four to
ferment in another town. Webster Grove:
Sleep tonight. The traveler must hurry home.

A Wandering Voice

A wandering voice
breezes by her ear.
Whispers of future beginnings
slide into sudden awareness,
then dangle there while she endeavors
to wrap her mind around dark riddles.

Sibyl, Sibyl, Sibyl streams like silver ribbons
across the labyrinth of ages.
When Alexander consulted Lamia's daughter
for legitimacy, she blessed his rise in Egypt.
Sambethe, Noah's girl, lies in Fresco
in the Sistine Chapel.
Now summer zephyrs stir an eager search,
a quest for answers to this puzzle of disturbance.

As the Sibyl of the Oracle raved her
prophecy at Delphi of Divine birth,
Michelangelo painted her image.
Raphael depicted angels as they
rendered their instructions
to sister Sibyls. Now it's but an Earth Mother of
lowly estate who is baffled by their predictions.

She inclines her head to allow mystifying words
full rein. Something there is that strikes a spark
on long-stifled embers.
With innate deliberation,
a dispelling breath,
that spark becomes one
with morning mist.
Its vapors curl along the dew of dawn,
search out receptive souls,
wandering, ever wandering.

A Memory

A memory of a dream—
no it's a prediction—
invades my mind as I turn to
leave the computer where I've labored
two hours since lunch in study—
reading *real* poets.
Through the window, spring birds fly back and forth
across the yard.
Down the street a large maple's top branches fan the air.
Purple flags line the other side of the
chain-link fence. I stare as each spot demands my attention—
try to recall that prediction. Will I learn the answer to it all?
Startling thick clouds—grey—pale—
hang low overhead. I long to plunge into them with
both arms up to my elbows.
There's a mystery to solve. I must dig.
Foolish nonsense—to dig into formless shapes for
answers to questions I cannot phrase. There's
a matter of some consequence I must
wrap my mind around to pass on a bit of intelligence.
Frustrated, I leave it all lying there
open-ended.

Beyond The Silence

Numbness begs at the rim of fire
that crackles at my core—
a dog panting to pounce on the roasted piece
materialized in chill silence.

Steadily it advances.

This is dying—surely—then
give me a reason to die.
Give me one word beyond the silence to
smother now smoldering coals.

Throw the dog his piece.

Dawning

I woke up warm and easy
Remembering music, a muted piano,
Fragments of conversation.
He has charm, that's what it is.
Was the voice my mother's?
You've always given in to charm.
Just remember what happened to the prizes
You won as a child.
Someone always got the best of you.
You'd end up with nothing.
I knew I had won.
I wish I could remember more of the dream.
It was his face, I was warm and
So outside myself, not touching anything.
The man has charm, that's all.
That music's still in my head.
The prize was mine to give, I won it, after all.
I still feel sleep-warm, and easy.
Or was the voice my own?

Down Water Street

beyond telephone wires on the other side
haphazard trumpet vines scramble to the tops of oak and maple
from sprawled out shrubs spread thirty feet across
mimicking an orange grove here in South Jersey.

Waxy white and purple spikes of orchid
reach toward them from their tan clay pots
here on my polished pine windowsill.

Nearly four this August afternoon, it's cooler now than it's been
since dawn, closing down the day a bit early. A few tired
    geese
honk their way west across the sky just this side of
heavy puffs of cloud pulling down one lonely patch of blue.

I stand in the doorway to watch their strain against the tide of the
west wind as they beat their way toward freshness of an
    inland lake.
Memory pictures endless flights of their long gone ancestral
    family
traveling this way how many Augusts ago? Fewer and fewer
    wing by
these days while my family grows wider each generation.

Today's children don't go to the door or out the door to watch
their passage. How can I tell them they must not miss it?

Birch Canoeist

Birch canoeist glides

Between cloud and deep river

Peers down, plumbs the sky.

A man like a tree

Nourished from above

Opens to Spring's seductive smile

Accepts her healing tears which

Thaw the frost of Winter's curse.

Black beads blinking

Sparrow pleads

From pointed finger of bony apple tree.

Grey mist implores with weeping of her own:

December, December with nights too long for sleeping

Be gone!

Decision

Another unwrapped gift of Time
spread here at my feet
oozes like extra virgin olive oil
poured out in generous globs,
sidles its way into my conscious awareness
ready for me to step into,
slide drunkenly in circles
from one untapped measure of
infinite potential
to yet another disclaimer of unleashed intent.
Steady—I must steady myself
against that wild drumbeat of
derision. Go no further
beats past my temple,
thrusts out my hands in a blind attempt
to push against the precipice so near.
I strain against each opposing force.
No longer shall I submit to doubt, to
threat of disdain, to standing alone on
sinking sand, the wild west wind
whipping strands of wet hair across my face.

Elegy For An Alien

Waves sigh and then retreat
Sigh and then retreat again
From migrant on November's beach
Alone absorbing salted air to
Purify the gloom within.

Travailing bird fly on, fly on.
The flock is gone. You are alone.
Rules change not for dove who low in
Wonder hovers, stayed by one who
Strength renewed, rejoins his own.

Preparing proper final rest
Blood red November sky draws down
Draws tight and deepens into gray to
Black to starless night to
Rise on barren dune, alien gone.

Contrail

There have been other crisp January days like this.
Only then the piercing blue sky was not crisscrossed by
Vapor trails. Those are not direct flight patterns up there from
New York to Miami or Philadelphia to Fort Worth.
They're playing up there. Look how they've zigzagged all
    over.
They must have been out before dawn to have the whole sky
Filled with their puffy water balloons already.

It used to be if you moved out of the city
The sky would amaze you the way it comes down to
Touch the earth all around. Down to the hills back there—
Down to the river over here. In the city
Factory smoke was what you called sky. The color of sky was
Grey. On sultry summer days, verdigris.

Here now the startling blue penetrates still—but in
Patches between the jets' chalked borderlines—
Divvied up into a piece of sky for that one and
Another piece for this—demanding acute
Vertical vision of sensible
Horizon-tuned eyes.

Dissection Of A Dream

I'm a used nun, she confided. Musing,
I tried pulling it apart. She didn't say I used to be a nun,
but I'm a used nun. How was she used? was my reaction.
And she is good. So she must have been used wisely
if that's really what she intended to say.

I wake from the dream, wander about all day,
try to picture who that was. It was so real.
I have good, good women friends.
Which one, I wonder, feels like a used nun?

Suddenly I grasp the spoken remark might have been
"none"—not "nun,"
in which case, aware of how dream-speech is slurred,
could have been "no one," swerved into "n'one."
So that's it! A bit of the puzzle falls into place.
Still: who is she? this used n'one—
Do we ever really know how a woman feels about herself?

Color Me Dawn

Color me Dawn.
Slide silver beams
along spider's leap

from Juniper branch
to amber frond

while I drink in
morning's greening.

Color me wonder with intake of breath.
Color me blessed beyond meaning.

Color me Dawn.

Slip slivers of dreams
between merging clouds—

conscious reminder of
time's ebb and flow—

pressing their presence
into my scheming.

Color me Daylight.
Dawn came but once.
Once I opened to New, overwhelming,
arms flung wide to beauty indwelling.

In dwelling between Dawn's remarkable thrust and
Day's soft continuum, its real line defined,

brings me that joy I crave to remember.
Color me Dawn—I refuse to surrender.

Norma Paul
April 12, 2012

Don't Ask

Don't ask me what this poem means to me.
Reading it silently or aloud
I feel its impact,
enter its every word,
wrap it around my shoulders,
plunge my hands into its meat,
push against it to free them,
shake off its empty syllables,
inhale its dust,
spit it out.

In no uncertain terms
this poem tells me
I know you.
I've been you.
I stand with you
on the measured plain
of your existence,
face to face,
eye to eye.

Essence

Extract one essence:
Unconcerned, cologne titillates
Intense, perfume reels.
Distill. Purify.
Cologne, carefree, caresses.
Perfume's volatile.

GROPING

Imagine then—
Venus
Close to Earth as
She's ever been—
In conjunction with
Mars—Jupiter—
the crescent Moon.
Imagine its
clear brightness
yearned for
here in Barnegat—while
    I peer into
      yet another night of
Cloud cover.

In Bed—and Out Again

Reheated tea . . .
not like tea at all
the rim of the mug cool to my lips.

Drain it. Drink in wariness
lest some not quite remembered
presence manifest itself
rushing past my ears.

Evocation

If you had not happened by?
A certain strain coaxed from an E string
Evokes this same sweep of fatal intent
Holds me poised in mid-flight
Hummingbird probing lily's throat.

In the end Destiny is one:
I am an entity
Swept into the breach by your
Startling grace or by
Weeping violin.

Half Moon

Peers in the window from the southern October sky

This seventh day of the tenth month

Promising familiar closeness through an

Untested search for liberation,

unbounded lightness of being, of newness

Once more to revel in its silver sphere

Once more to sing through hesitating dance steps

Into claimed delight.

Moonglow lights the way to autonomy of spirit

Madcap revelry

Simplicity of self.

Flooding freely the widening space

unfenced silver light spreads its radiant pool.

In The Middle of March

In the middle of March
fat mourning doves were
back to search out nesting areas
from high wires—
destined again to select
low ground
subject to invasion by
prowling felines
but programmed to return to
danger like their forbears.
I wanted to shoo them
from my yard where the
chain link fence that keeps in
Jak, the friendly Schnauzer
would not prevent a
marauding cat from
sneaking in for a
midnight feast. Somehow
doves seem to think the
overgrown grapevine will
shield their progeny. It must be
they have no memory of
last spring's pitiful loss
else why would they once again
tempt fate?

But then Spring Break
finds moms and dads financing
begged-for trips to Cancun.
Would you call them bird-brained?

Finis

We heard its thud on tinted glass.
A cloud shaded your eyes. I walked by.
Are you going to leave it there? You asked and
cradling the bird in both your hands, set it to the side.

Bringing water in a cup, you pried its beak for
drops that spilled right out. With averted glance
you left it under the Cedar and
took a long time washing your hands.

How soon your softness turns brittle
witless bird! embracing doom which
beckoned with an image of your own desire
shy hovering would have shown.

How can you be so hard? You asked on your return.
It happens all the time, I answered, you get numb.

Hungry Cat

"Absurd," they say, "to spoil an alley cat
The way you do," when they come downstairs
To find me waiting for the coffee to perk,
Telling them the cat was hungry and
Since it was almost light out I may as well stay up.

Poor cat. But who else can I blame
When this longing ends sleep and
Hangs my feelings on an attic clothesline
To dry stiff, wringer creases left unstirred?

Grace

Grace, oh Grace, oh Saving Grace
Enfold me, sweep me into your long-abiding presence
Without question.
Let my tears flow—
Dry—
Well up once more for every wrong.
I confess my crashing downfall—
My wretched run from your
Wondrous peace—
Unbelieving
Doubting.
Then, finally then, from the bottom of the mud-dark abyss
Remembrance.
I reach
Grasp
Catch my breath
Overwhelmed by sustenance
Instilled within my troubled soul
Bringing light
Brilliant light
To flood each dark depression
To answer this petition.

Imprint

She lay on his side of the bed
night after hollow night,
first to reclaim remembered warmth,
togetherness, peace that filled them
as they held each other.

Early days alone she reached for comfort
in this manner. It allowed her to survive
Spring's arrival when robin's song
left her bawling.

As one year slides into the next
his legacy worms its way
into her bones.
Decisions once delayed catapult her
hesitance into bold resolution.
Once a heedless follower
leadership becomes her mien.
Today her brow, unruffled,
precedes her forward thrust.

Insistent

The three o'clock hour
Pushes into my dream state
Grabs it out of my hands
Up you must be up.

There just behind your eyes there is a
Jewel to pluck from that knowing state
You have been desperate to mine.
Now is the time to dig away at the
Scrabble enclosing a copious gem.

Receptive
I incline my entire being toward
Revelation I cannot fathom.
Mockery envelops me.

It's One Of . . .

It's one of those Saturdays
you don't want to get out of your robe
no matter how late you lay in bed
contemplating accomplishments
you ticked off on the fingers of
both hands
to get through before lunch.
It started off with putting on the kettle
for tea. Just too much of an effort
to make coffee. Then, forget oatmeal.
Spread a slice of toast with
peanut butter, instead. Of course,
you have to fill a bag with groceries
for the mailman to pick up today.
Haphazardly, you pick out a can of
tuna, a carton of chicken broth,
that bag of grits you don't know why
you have, the condensed milk you needed
to make coconut macaroons
which you never got coconut for.
So out you go to the mailbox
in your robe
with the note you're sending to Maureen.
You think, wow, I'd lose all her respect
if she could see me now
nearly ten in the morning
no shower yet
no makeup
out in the neighborhood.

Late August

Late August
Down Route Nine lace has
draped itself over every trace of
greenery from Barnegat to Little Egg Harbor
a softening veil against the brash thrust of
summer's flagrant forestation.
It's time once again for calm reflexion
for stilling one's senses
within an island of contentment
for drawing in a deep breath of
pine-scented deliverance
for closing one's self into an
indelible stance of solitary enlightenment
for speaking farewell to midsummer.
Nothing else.

It's too soon to greet the morrow.
    Wind down.

Inversion

Looking back I peer through the wrong end of the
telescope everything is small far away un
reachable not easy to detect my arms use
less unable to grasp hold tense I would
have to let go of today in order to re
treat to find out exactly what I was
immersed in but unwilling to let
go because then I would be fall
ing falling into dark depths I
covered over long since.

Lemon Moon

Save me a slice of the Lemon Moon
filmy fulgent Lemon Moon
translucent sweet tart
chilled in lucid night.
Surfeited by fumy hyacinth
jaded by lilac's oppressive breath
my flagging appetite quickens at
Lemon Moon's freshening light.

Legacy

A man grieves when he examines his inheritance
Meager results of his father's struggle to
Secure a hold on the skidding crust. He stands—
Presses his fingertips into his temples
Contemplates whether to turn the soil
Along this furrow—or lean the hoe
Worn smooth and gray
Against the shade tree in the center of the field
And walk away.

It's Already April

Where's my spring-inspired vision?
The new Japanese Cherry on the other side of
Ridgeway Street is all decked out in feathery pink
but my heart does not sing.

We walked to the creek—the boys and I—
where they tossed in stones, watched the water
push out splashing circles to startle frogs.
No frogs croaked their April greetings.

TV announcers foretell eighty degrees.
A serious sky, gritty gray,
hides the sun. Everything's
holding its breath. Are you there, friend?
We're all in this together.

Send me a shot of fresh air, won't you?
It's already April.

Jubilate

Prim, rose of early spring's formal cultivated bed
Pales as autumn's gaudy herald Goldenrod
Shouts boisterous from the roadside
Offends the sensitive
Startles dormant crickets into exuberant chorus!

It's Long Past Dusk

My juices begin to flow now; stirrings
chase each other within my breast—
in a longing need for answers.
I search a higher form of Truth from my
Consciousness. There is something concrete to get hold of there
that will not come to the surface.

I delve deeper within the existence I recognize.

If I keep coming back, keep looking into
the familiar, will the New appear to answer the riddle invading
    my senses?

It's slippery territory here.

If I look away I'll lose it.

Jumping Jack

Blow me that sweet breath of spring.
Airy portent of summer fog sways on a bough above.
A jack jumps on hot pavement when
A small hand tosses up a blue sphere.
It lands . . . bounces . . . is swept up with the
Sharp hot star star star—one then two then three.
The jack waits for the sweep—sings along the pavement
Makes its mark as it scrapes along—
Swept up—flung down.
Twirls away, away, and away.

Life Continues

Blessings surround me—

matriarch in a patriarch society—

where men struggle to maintain
their hold on the skidding crust of
autonomy—

fiercely insist on their personal portion of
coffee and cigarettes from Wawa—

while their wives are left to deal with
everyday concerns sweeping in around the
home, its tidy frame wrapped about the picture to
present to the world at large, her requirement to fill the
young ones with generous meals of good health,
clothe them in suitable outfits and their
allotment of vitamins and self-esteem.

It's a daily routine
dealt with in a daily manner.
It all adds up to "Life
continues."

Mimosa In November

Long seedpods hang dry from
sere bent branches where fragrant
beckoning blossoms enticed the
sweet-craving hummingbird our
last July.

Remember how hummingbird hovers—
its wings in constant motion.
It fills its need with the swiftness of light
then speeds on to flash its beauty
for another's eyes.

Don't mourn our loss.
I can't mourn our loss.
Rejoice that we held tight the passion
satisfied with the eager lift of
showy pom-pom amid arching branches.

Memory retains the whelming scent
all through November's clouded passage.

Neighbors Gardening

Pat waters butterfly bush, azalea.
A fresh sweet odor
seeps in through closed window.

On my side of the fence
a rose grows wild—deep red,
smallish, unplanted
unplanned bonus of spring.

With a deep breath of dew, I
turn back to my search for
just the right word,
inhale deeply, begin.

Long Arc Of The Universe

How long ago did Martin state
with firm belief in future good

the Arc of the Moral Universe
Bends toward Justice?

How fitting it is that such bending is
resolved by the stance held by

yet another deprived citizen
who now declares for freedom of choice

in each private decision.
Laws enacted to restrict such choice

cannot stand. We must take hold of
our freedom, each of us,

you for yours, me for mine—
freedom to marry, freedom to refrain,

freedom to parent, freedom to abstain.
Cast aside conformity unchosen

in hair, in dress, in demeanor.
Live up to potential inborn or discovered.

Proceed on the path to peace,
uncovered.

Music Is The Space

If music is the space between the notes,
per Claude Debussy,
then poetry is the pause between the words
we struggle to create
to wrap around each poignant emotion
that floods our being with yearning.
It compels us to offer up our meager sense of
self-unpolished, incapable of any act of heroics.
Take us as you find us. We cannot be other.
I place one heartfelt esthetic before you
to await your recognition. Parse each phrase,
then set the piece apart on the shelf of your
conscious awareness.
Walk away from it.
Come back to let it all sink in.
Pause. Re-read. Pause again.
This is poetry.

On The Front Porch In The Sun

This May morning—warm—warm—faces upturned—
Eyes closed—receive a benediction. Low, a dove mourns.
Mother's Day azaleas deck the railing—
Grass smooth from Saturday's mowing—
Cardinals—robins vie for airplay. A lone bee
Zigzags in his droning quest for territory.
Hear the dove mourn.

One holiday gone, speak of the next—that
Awkward pause in another year of inhumanity.
Decorate the long-remembered. But for one
Who lies in unknown ground from an
Unforgiving time when youth wronged
Would not compromise perceived justice.

Now taste salt in daily bread—brood over
Headlines that underscore bitter penchant for
Vengeance. Plant a crimson azalea beside one
Grave-marked flag. Wait for
Taps' final plaintive descent.

Memory's Currency

Has been revaluated.
Turn in hoarded gold for
Cash and carry certificates.

Now and then
Treasure lost in the transfer
Will be caught out of the
Corner of your eye

Distant sparks from a shooting star.

That lump in your throat
Will be dulled with the
Passing of time.

Invitation

MY HOUSE IS LARGE THOUGH MY HOUSE IS SMALL

Windows are not dressed to hide its
open rooms with dog-eared books
on tables by each chair.

A kettle's always ready to brew
a cuppa, should that be your need,
to perk up your spirits when down
while we spell out your conflicts to solve.

You'll find you're not required to converse
if you'd rather be still. Just sit back,
drink in the quiet. Let it wash over you.
Close your eyes.

With the spirit of peace in this small house,
you don't have to try to impress.
It's cozy but will not suppress you.
Be bold as you wish. Be free.

If no one's home, just venture in
for a calming breath to fill your need.
Slip into an inviting chair, lose your shoes,
put up your feet.

Singing Sands

Returning to the Upper Peninsula of my birth
on the shore of Lake Superior
we listened to the pink singing sands—marveled that it was true.
We heard them sing without words—a long unending tune
in the key of C I think. Or E. Or from one to the other,
but smoothly so you couldn't say where C ended and E began.
It may be the reason my mother obtained for me a violin
when I told her quite clearly I wanted to play a Hawaiian guitar.
I had heard it—the Hawaiian guitar—on the radio and
knew it was for me. But mama had access to a violin
through one of her many cousins in Michigan.
When it came in its odd case that opened on the end,
not horizontally like every other violin case,
I was even more nonplused, aside from the fact that
it was a violin, not a guitar, Hawaiian or otherwise.
With the bow there was a small cake of rosin.
I was shown how to rosin the bow, then tighten it
until it was taut enough to produce sound on the strings—
    g, d, a, e—
Before many days I grew to cherish that violin,
the sounds that trilled along my ribs as I stood
sliding the whitened bow down in one strong sweep
then up in a languorous reach. I practiced,

oh how I practiced in an effort to bring forth real music,
to reach that epitome of graceful accomplishment,
to gratify my patient teacher,
to astound my doubting mother who knew
my heart was in the Hawaiian guitar.
Along the way, I forged a bond with destiny.
As years slide by, I step with confidence into
every unplanned, unanticipated byroad within the maze
revealed day by day, each year, through each turn in
Life's ontology. Today, without a violin, its memory
sings within my being, pink sands of yesterday
transformed.

Step Out!

Take the measure of the morning.
Cherry red feathers release their
Grip on maple branches that
Scrape against early fog.
Tendrils uncurl—
Plummet to pool in a gathering of
Beet red—delicacy distorted.

Take the measure of the pines.
Inhale their pungent shadows before they
Burn dry, de-scented.
Stretch wide the tape:
Take the measure of the day.
Embrace the morning. Gather it as firewood.
Grasp a maple to scrape away the fog.

Something of My Mind and Thought

Something of my mind and thought
to last beyond my three score years and ten,
or however long that turns out to be . . .
I marvel at Christo and Jeanne Claude
who spent hours, days, years in the planning and
execution, only to dismantle in the end.
Nothing's left to see—no gauzy textiles
hanging above a river in the windswept Rockies.
No gates unfurled through Central Park,
appreciated by how few dwellers, visitors there.
Nothing to hold in two hands,
nothing to curl up with when winds howl about the house,
when grey clouds touch earth on a November afternoon.

To clasp close to your breast the wondering
redemption left behind—how can they be so blasé?
To light a match—see it flicker—spark an un-held-onto.
Down in the river canoeists will marvel, rafters concentrate
on the rapids before them. Unable to look up, they will miss it.

If you read this
years from now, you'll miss my attempts, too.
They'll slip from your fingers, slip from your grasp
of my particular intellect.

Christo's right! You can only do what you
must for yourself. Whoever is on the
outside looking in cannot matter.
Matter is but a figment of your own
sphere of influence—elusive.

That's the beauty of it all.
There's nothing for you, stranger, to hold onto,
streaming through my consciousness
so quickly I cannot grasp myself, myself.
Oh, Whitman, now I know
what you were trying to tell us—swirling by—
oh love—love it is. We feel it long before
we find it in our midst—in our nature—
in the dream of Life—in this dream of life—
in this dream.

The Keen Edge Of Truth

Stepping across my Rubicon to a point of no return
Takes me under a leaden sky to a dark dark wood,
branches curving down to prevent clear vision.
What lies ahead can only be surmised by one who
passed this way before. Press on, I demand.
Reach deep into your center. Carry it forward into
unknown dark to stamp out fallen yearnings
or turn back now until you reach that
determinate clutch of caring.
But no. Keep on. Search to uncover hidden bounty.
Prized gems await your driven reach.
Peer into unrelenting night.
Blackness imprisons all but remembrance.
I thrust the essence of my being into remembrance.
Light slants across the periphery of my vision
revealing the keen edge of Truth.
Straining to grasp the whole of it, I hurl mind and soul
in one compressed unity
into that revelation, inviting destruction—
surely destruction.
Incredibly, unity survives. Light is restored.
In Truth then is survival. In Truth alone is survival.

Tempered Vision

There was a time I volunteered at county social services
to spend my lunch hours, wearing the county-supplied
I.D. badge, running errands for a blinded man who lived in a
trailer park off Route 9.

A "blind rep" had schooled him in the safest method to light the
pilot on his kitchen range, the steps to count from table to
refrigerator, the hand-holds to reach for when stepping out or in.

Henry, when we met, displayed jaundiced defeat toward his ex.
She bade him leave their residence the day they burned the
    mortgage.
Just can't abide that stumbling in the dark, she told him.
Fighting a cold, he held tissues up to his clouded eyes.

It was a pretty easy assignment. Once a week I would
    complete his banking.
Shopping, I followed his list of preferred groceries and put
    them away
when I returned to his trailer.
Informed that diabetes had led to his blindness, I tried to
    sneak in whole grain
in place of the Wonder bread specified,
picked out two percent dairy instead of whole milk,
"forgot" requested chocolate chip cookies,
substituted peaches in natural juice for heavy syrup.

As November drew close to the holidays, Henry whined for
   pumpkin pie and
chocolate pudding with whipped cream. Real, he said, don't
   spend my money
on any of that fake stuff. O.K., Henry, I complied.
But after his bitter memories welled up, distrust of women
   spilled over into
Henry's first holiday on his own. I think you've done enough,
   he said.
I'll get my buddy to help me out now.
After that, I turned in my badge, shied away from
volunteering person-to-person.

. . . *The Speaker Declared*
A Clock

Could be fashioned of rain in a bucket.
Just see how many drops fall in an hour, say.
Then multiply those inches as they increase and
You can tell how long it came down.

What of my outpour?
My bucket is empty.
The sun rose the sun set the moon rose
Yet time is immeasurable.

It feels like rain but there's
Nothing to show for it.

The Brave Man When He's Hurt

Will take a deep drag on his pain
Until it fills his chest and
Fills his lungs and fills his head—
Only then to release his grip
In an effort to dispel the dark power
Like smoke on air.